D0116696

God's Great News for Children
Leading Your Child to Christ

Written by Rick Osborne & Marnie Wooding

TYNDALE

Tyndale House Publishers, Wheaton, Illinois

Heritage Builders®

God's Great News for Children: Leading Your Child to Christ
Copyright © 2002 by Rick Osborne & Marnie Wooding
All rights reserved. International copyright secured.

ISBN: 1-56179-971-8

A Focus on the Family Book published by
Tyndale House Publishers, Wheaton, Illinois.

Unless otherwise noted, Scripture quotations are from the *Holy Bible, New International Version®*. Copyright © 1973, 1978, 1984 by International Bible Society. Used by permission of Zondervan Publishing House. All rights reserved.
Scripture quotations marked (KJV) are taken from the *King James Version*.
Scripture quotations marked (NKJV) are taken from the *New King James Version*. Copyright © 1982 by Thomas Nelson, Inc. Used by permission. All rights reserved.
Scripture quotations marked (NASB) are taken from the *New American Standard Bible* 1960, 1962, 1963, 1968, 1971, 1972, 1973, 1975, 1977, 1995 by the Lockman Foundation. Used by permission. (www.Lockman.org).

Focus on the Family books are available at special quantity discounts when purchased in bulk by corporations, organizations, churches, or groups. Special imprints, messages, and excerpts can be produced to meet your needs. For more information, contact: Resource Sales Group, Focus on the Family, 8605 Explorer Drive, Colorado Springs, CO 80920; or phone (800) 932-9123.

No part of this publication may be reproduced, stored in a retrieval system, or transmitted in any form or by any means—electronic, mechanical, photocopy, recording, or otherwise—without prior permission of the publisher.

Library of Congress Cataloging-in-Publication Data

Cover Design: Candi Park D'Agnese
Illustrations: Ed Olson
Key Painter: Mike Inman
Additional Painting: Curt Walstead
Desktop Publishing: Andrew Jaster
Proofreading: Rosalie Krusemark

Printed in Italy
2 3 4 5 6 7 8 9 / 08 07 06 05 04

Table of Contents

Introduction

Many parents wonder how to help their children build a lasting relationship with Jesus. The first step in any relationship is an introduction. Children learn about relationships by watching their parents interact with others. Including your children in your relationship with Jesus is the first step. Going to church, praying as a family, and reading the Bible are the fundamental building blocks of introducing Jesus to your child. Sharing your relationship with God demonstrates that God is an important part of your life. Jesus is part of your family.

Each child's growing relationship with Jesus is as unique and individual as your child. Exploring the gospel with each of your children will never be the same experience twice. Some children become Christians through Sunday school, some at summer camp, some through their parents, some on their own through prayer, and so on.

You can play a part in leading your child to Jesus by sharing the gospel story with him or her, and by creating opportunities to talk about Jesus. There's no need to push. Just tell the story and show your children who Jesus is. Learning about someone is the second step in any relationship.

When you're reading the story of Jesus with your children, use the opportunity to tell them about what Jesus has done for them. Discuss everyday events and relate them back to the message of Jesus. Don't forget to make time for questions after sharing a gospel story. You'll be surprised at what your children will teach you as you both explore the answers.

Use daily opportunities to explore Jesus' character. When your child feels guilty about something he or she has done, talk about forgiveness. Or in the grocery store, talk about God's generosity and love. There are no textbook answers to sharing the gospel with your child. God will provide you those moments to share because He wants your child to come to Him even more than you do. Relax, God is on your side.

You can create an atmosphere in your homes where learning about Jesus is just part of your lives anytime and anywhere. Reading the gospel with your child can be as easy as sharing the family photo album. Each gospel story is like a photograph that reveals Jesus' character and His love for us. Go ahead and open the gospel and explore that very family experience which is Jesus' story.

A Friend Forever

Imagine a best friend who is always there, always ready to listen to you, and always ready to help out. Jesus wants to be that kind of a friend to you. In fact He wants to be your best friend and, most importantly, a friend forever. Friendships grow strongest when you take the time to learn about the other person. But, how well do you know Jesus? Learning more about Him is as easy as picking up a very special book. Reading the Bible is like opening a window that looks back at the things Jesus did. The more you know about what He did, the better you get to know Him. Let's start getting to know Jesus by looking back to the very beginning of the world.

When God created everything, He wasn't alone. Not at all! Jesus was with His Father from the very first. *"He was with God in the beginning" (John 1:2).* So was the Holy Spirit. The Bible tells us the Holy Spirit is the Spirit of God.

Now God had a tremendously huge idea, absolutely the biggest, grandest idea that ever was, and Jesus was all part of that amazing event called creation. Let's take a look at God's big galaxy-sized steps in making the world.

Begin at the Beginning

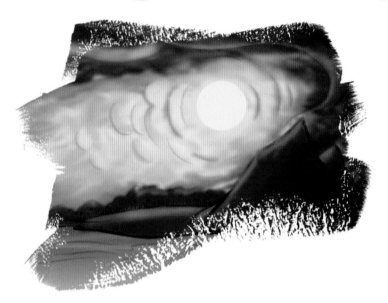

an you picture in your mind darkness that is blacker than any dark you can think of—blacker than when you close your eyes, or stand in a closed closet? From this big black space of nothingness the Father, His Son, Jesus, and the Holy Spirit created heaven and the earth. *"God, said, 'Let there be light.' And there was light" (Genesis 1:3).* When God talks things definitely start happening! He called the light day and the darkness night. That was day one of everything.

The second day God began to create a space to put everything in, or on, or between, or around. God separated water from the air. *"God called the huge space 'sky'" (Genesis 1:8).*

7

So, by day two there was water and there was air. But what else would God need?

On day three, for the very first time ever, thundering ocean waves rolled and crashed onto brand new untouched beaches. That's right, God made land. *"God called the dry ground 'land.' He called the waters that were gathered together 'oceans.' And God saw that it was good"* (Genesis 1:10). From mountaintop to deep ocean bottom, God sculpted it all with a whisper of His word. This was the landscape of God's earthly creation. Now it was time for God to fill in the details. And what amazing details were to come?

God is the master gardener. He clothed His undressed land with plants of every kind and description. *"The land*

produced plants. Each kind of plant had its own kind of seeds (Genesis 1:12). By creating seeds, God made sure that His garden would continue to grow and grow and grow. Each seed contained the next baby plant in a never ending chain. The deserts were filled with cactus; rich valleys full of tall grasses; and mountains thick with magnificent pine trees. God had designed Earth to be a perfect garden.

Day four in God's big plan was very special. *"God made two great lights. He made the larger light to rule over the day. He made the smaller light to rule over the night. He also made the stars (Genesis 1:16).* God made the sun and the moon. Jesus saw the very first sunrise! A bold orange sun rising on the horizon to bring morning to a sleepy new world! How about the first night sky filled with a glowing moon and galaxies full of stars? Amazing! But why was God doing this miracle? Can you guess?

The next day God created all creatures that swim. The oceans, lakes, and rivers were filled with life from the biggest whales to the tiniest shrimp. Just like the oceans, the air was also filled with birds of every shape and kind. That's a whole lot of scales and feathers! God sure was...creative! But day six was to be the most important.

Then, God created all the animals that lived on the land. Animals that would race, prowl, and crawl through God's amazing garden. God made and put animals in their proper place until every nook and cranny on our planet had just the right amount.

Why did God do all these astounding things? The answer to that question can be found in God's most precious creation. On that very important sixth day, God created a man named Adam and a woman named Eve. Unlike anything else God created, He made people different, separate, and special. You see, God is so kind and loving that He wanted to make somebody to love and care for. *"Then God said, 'Let us make man in our likeness. Let them rule over the fish in the waters and the birds of the air. Let them rule over the livestock and over the whole earth'"* (Genesis 1:26).

Now do you know why God created such a wonderful, amazing, spectacular, absolutely sensational place? This world was His gift to His new family: Adam and Eve.

Or put another way US! That's right! God made us to be His children. And like a good father, God loves us with all His heart and wants us to love Him just the same way. Remember that Jesus has always been with God and He has been helping take care of the world from day one.

LET'S TALK:
On days when we may feel ordinary and not very special at all, remember we are part of God's family and that makes us very important and special in His eyes. Just like Adam and Eve. What are some of your favorite things God has created?

Don't Talk to Strangers!

It's morning in God's brand new garden. The Garden of Eden was a wonderful place to be! A bright morning sun rose over a dusky hill chasing the nighttime shadows away. The waking birds fluttered and chirped in the treetops. The bees flew out of the hives in search of sweet flowers. The larger animals stirred and called to each other. Life was perfect and easy under God's care because He is a good and loving Father. And every day Adam and Eve lived happy and took care of the garden just as God wanted them to.

There was one very important thing that Adam and Eve had to remember. God said, *"You can eat the fruit of any tree*

*that is in the garden.
But you must not eat the
fruit of the tree of the
knowledge of good and evil. If
you do, you can be sure that
you will die" (Genesis 2:16–17).*
That wasn't such a hard rule
because God had provided an entire produce section of different foods to eat like fruits, nuts, berries, and yes...even
vegetables.

But, little did Eve know she was being watched by a
tricky troublemaker. A snake in more ways than one. He had

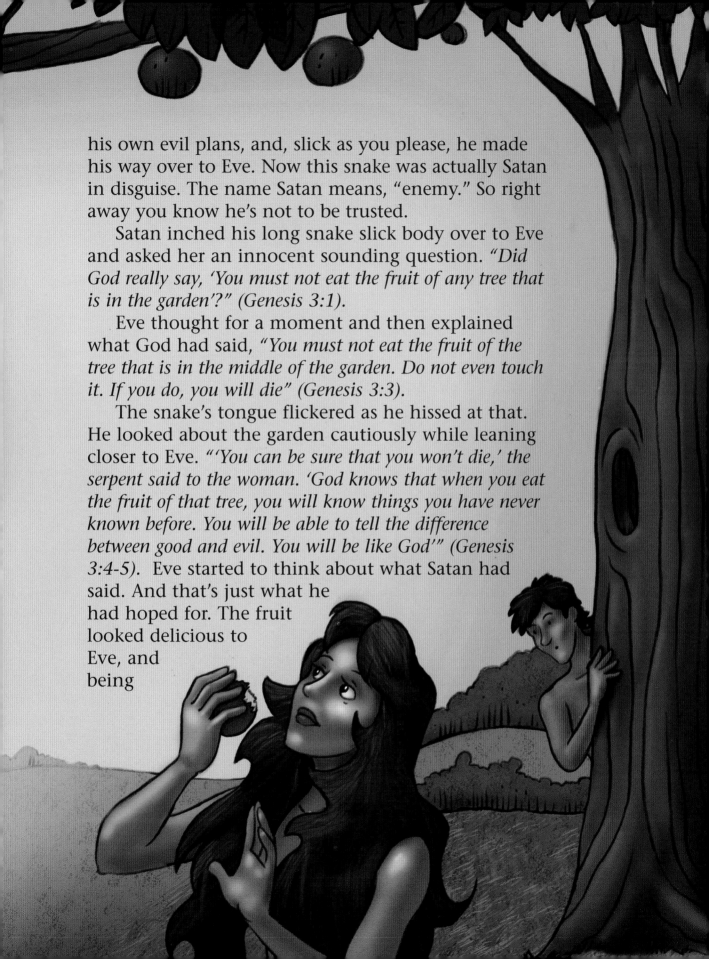

his own evil plans, and, slick as you please, he made his way over to Eve. Now this snake was actually Satan in disguise. The name Satan means, "enemy." So right away you know he's not to be trusted.

Satan inched his long snake slick body over to Eve and asked her an innocent sounding question. *"Did God really say, 'You must not eat the fruit of any tree that is in the garden'?" (Genesis 3:1).*

Eve thought for a moment and then explained what God had said, *"You must not eat the fruit of the tree that is in the middle of the garden. Do not even touch it. If you do, you will die" (Genesis 3:3).*

The snake's tongue flickered as he hissed at that. He looked about the garden cautiously while leaning closer to Eve. *"'You can be sure that you won't die,' the serpent said to the woman. 'God knows that when you eat the fruit of that tree, you will know things you have never known before. You will be able to tell the difference between good and evil. You will be like God'" (Genesis 3:4-5).* Eve started to think about what Satan had said. And that's just what he had hoped for. The fruit looked delicious to Eve, and being

smart like God seemed like a good thing too. Why would the snake lie? But! That's just how Satan operates...he seems to have all the answers, but the truth is he's steering you in the wrong direction.

Eve took the fruit from the tree and ate it. Then she gave some to Adam. Their world would never be the same. Adam and Eve disobeyed God and took a big step away from God's will. The snake had lied, of course; the fruit didn't make them smart like God; it just made them disobedient and separate from Him.

God was walking through the garden calling for Adam and Eve. *"Where are you?" (Genesis 3:9).* But they were so frightened and ashamed, they hid from Him. God knew what was up and questioned them. Adam answered, *"It was the woman you put here with me. She gave me some fruit from the tree. And I ate it" (Genesis 3:12).* Eve said, *"The serpent tricked me. That's why I ate the fruit" (Genesis 3:13).* How could Adam and Eve have made such a huge mistake? They didn't trust God to know what was best for them.

Adam and Eve had put their own will before God's and now everything changed. Their actions had built a wall of sin between them and their heavenly Father. God had to send them out of His wonderful garden.

God still loved them very much, but because Adam and Eve had sinned, sin became part of them. It was like sin had put a hurt or scar on their spirit that would never go away. Even Adam and Eve's children would carry that sin scar and be born apart from God. And so would their children and so on, all the way to us today. It would seem Satan had scored a big-time victory! He had managed to separate humans from their heavenly Father.

So is that it? The end of the story? Are people always going to be separated from God? No! Even though God hates sin, He loves us! He had a plan to help people get free of sin and come back to Him again. God the Father would send His Son, Jesus, into the world to wipe away the damage that Satan had done. How? The first part of the answer can be found in a little village many, many years after Adam and Eve lived on the earth.

LET'S TALK:

What would the world be like today if Adam and Eve had never sinned? Probably like heaven on Earth! Life would be full of the good things God created for us without anything being sad, bad, or evil. Try to describe what your life would be like.

It's Time!

I t was a hot, lazy day in Nazareth; the potters were pounding and mixing clay; shepherds were tending their herds; and young boys were fidgeting in their seats learning their lessons in the small synagogue. A young woman named Mary was going about her daily chores perhaps fetching water from the well or weeding her family's herb garden. It was a busy and exciting time for Mary because very soon she was to be married to a young man named Joseph. But that wasn't the only exciting thing that was about to happen to Mary.

It was time for God to send His Son, Jesus, to Earth. So He sent a very special angel named Gabriel with an

extremely important message. In fact Gabriel's name means "God is Mighty." That is a great name for a great angel.

Suddenly the angel Gabriel appeared right in front of Mary. She was startled by this surprise visit. He said, *"The Lord has given you special favor. He is with you"* (Luke 1:28). This greeting puzzled her, but Gabriel quickly befriended her, *"Do not be afraid, Mary. God is very pleased with you"* (Luke 1:30). It was very odd but somehow this stranger made Mary feel safe.

Gabriel said, *"You will become pregnant and give birth to a son. You must name him Jesus. He will be great and will be called the Son of the Most High God"* (Luke 1:31–32). This certainly wasn't your everyday message!

Mary was to have a baby that was God's Son! She wondered at how this could all happen? Gabriel was patient and explained. But would Mary have the faith to believe these amazing things to come?

Mary's answer was one full of love for God, *"'I serve the Lord,' Mary answered. 'May it happen to me just as you said it would'"* (Luke 1:38).

When Joseph heard

that Mary was going to have a baby he wasn't pleased at all. He hadn't seen Gabriel and didn't know what to believe. He even thought about breaking off his engagement with her.

But one night while Joseph slept, an angel appeared in his dream. *"Joseph, son of David, don't be afraid to take Mary home as your wife. The baby inside her is from the Holy Spirit. She is going to have a son. You must give him the name Jesus. That is because he will save his people from their sins"* (Matthew 1:20–21). Well, that dream was a real eye-opener! Joseph believed the messenger and took Mary home as his wife.

Just before Jesus was to be born, the government that ruled the land ordered everyone to go to his or her hometown to be counted. Joseph put Mary on his donkey and set out on the long journey to his boyhood home of Bethlehem. They traveled a rugged, dusty country road through steep hills, winding valleys, and rocky creeks.

Finally Mary and Joseph arrived, only to find the town bursting with strangers, like themselves, all trying to find a place to sleep for

the night. Poor Mary had realized miles back that the baby would be born that very day. A worried Joseph knocked on door after door, only to be turned away. There was no room for them anywhere. At long last Joseph was offered a clean stable for Mary to have her baby. And so in a small stable, which was probably filled with slumbering animals, God's only Son came to the world He helped create, as a tiny little baby.

Not too far away shepherds sat by their fires in fields near Bethlehem. The sounds of the sheep rustling in the dark, the flutter of bats as they flew low over the fields, and the crackle of the fire mixed with their talk. Suddenly the night sky exploded into brilliant light, *"An angel of the Lord*

appeared to them. And the glory of the Lord shone around them. They were terrified" (Luke 2:9). The shepherds blinked in complete surprise! They were terrified!

The calming angel spoke, *"Do not be afraid. I bring you good news of great joy. It is for all the people. Today in the town of David a Savior has been born to you. He is Christ the Lord"* *(Luke 2:10–11).* Then an entire choir of angels appeared singing praises to God! What an awesome birth announcement! Then the angel told the shepherds where to find this special baby.

The shocked shepherds were quick to spread the word, and soon people eager to see this new king surrounded the stable. It was a real celebration!

Jesus' birth was the most important day in human history. Because He is God's Son He was born without sin in His heart. Jesus Himself had come to make a way for all of us to be with God again.

LET'S TALK:
Christmas is a time we celebrate Jesus' birth. What are some of the things you like about Christmas?

Jesus' Journey

esus spent much of His growing up in the little town of Nazareth. Like any young boy, Jesus lived in a house with His family and went to school at the village synagogue, which was like a church. Joseph was a carpenter and he taught Jesus how to make things with wood.

No doubt Jesus' teacher or rabbi often told stories about Jerusalem. And each boy dreamed of one day walking the streets of the biggest city in all the land: Jerusalem with its markets bursting with strange and wonderful things from all over the world…Egypt, Greece, or even Rome. For village boys the most exciting part of Jerusalem was the temple

where people went to worship God. It was a special place as grand and wonderful as any king's palace! You can well imagine Jesus' excitement when He found out He was going to the most marvelous, wondrous, holiest place in the entire world—JERUSALEM.

"Every year Jesus' parents went to Jerusalem for the Passover Feast. When he was 12 years old, they went up to the Feast as usual" (Luke 2:41–42). The Passover was a very important Jewish holiday celebrating how God saved and rescued them from Egypt. The holiday lasted eight days, and during a celebration dinner, special foods were served and prayers of thanksgiving were prayed. Then the story of the exciting Exodus out of Egypt was retold.

The family journeyed through the lively streets of the city, and it seemed no matter where you were in Jerusalem you could see the shining white walls of the temple. Jesus' first visit to the temple must have been the most exciting day of His life so far. A steady stream of hundreds of people and animals flowed constantly in and out of the gates. Inside, the temple was a maze of courtyards and wide stone terraces. Tall, white, stone columns stood guard along the covered walkways. And everywhere seemed to shine with gold decorations.

Once inside, the very building seemed alive with music and the voices of hundreds of people singing, praying, and talking. People came to the temple to worship and also to listen to teachers talk about God. Twelve-year-old Jesus explored the temple with a growing sense of excitement. This was His Father's house! During the day, Jesus may have found a quiet place to listen to the teachers talk about God and His laws. Jesus absorbed every word they said. Each day His family was in Jerusalem, Jesus woke early and rushed back to the temple. But His first visit was over far to quickly, and soon it was time to return to Nazareth.

"After the Feast was over, his parents left to go back home. The boy Jesus stayed behind in Jerusalem. But they were unaware of it. They thought he was somewhere in their group. So, they traveled on for a day.

Then they began to look for him among their relatives and friends" (Luke 2:43–44). Jesus was nowhere to be found. Where was He? His worried parents turned around and headed back to the city.

Poor Mary and Joseph searched the streets of Jerusalem. They probably asked hundreds of people if they had seen a lost boy. With each passing day, they got more anxious. Where was Jesus?

"After three days they found him in the temple courtyard. He was sitting with the teachers. He was listening to them and asking them questions. Everyone who heard him was amazed at how much he understood. They also were amazed at his answers" (Luke 2:46–47). Even as a boy, Jesus' wisdom and knowledge of God stood out in a crowd.

"When his parents saw him, they were amazed. His mother said to him, 'Son, why have you treated us like this? Your father and I have been worried about you. We have been looking for you everywhere.' 'Why were you looking for me?' he asked. 'Didn't you know I had to be in my Father's house?' But they did not understand what he meant by that" (Luke 2:48–50). Jesus already understood His special relationship with His heavenly Father. He wasn't trying to be disobedient or thoughtless to His earthly parents. He loved them very much. But He seemed almost puzzled that they didn't naturally know He'd be found in the temple discussing the wonders of His Father. Where else would He be?

Jesus went home filled with the memories of His great adventures, and His parents filled with relief. *"Then he went*

back to Nazareth with them, and he obeyed them. But his mother kept all these things like a secret treasure in her heart. Jesus became wiser and stronger. He also became more and more pleasing to God and to people" (Luke 2:51–52).

LET'S TALK:

Jesus worked very hard at pleasing His parents. He was obedient and learned His lessons both at school and at home. He also spent important time learning about God and making time for God in His life. How can you be more like Jesus as you're growing up?

River's Edge

About twenty years later after Jesus had grown up, *"A man came who was sent from God. His name was John (John 1:6).* John was the same age as Jesus, and he loved and served God his whole life. But John wasn't an ordinary man. He didn't act or dress like the most trendy temple goers. No trendy robes for him. He wore rough camel hair clothes and he lived in the desert.

Few people would have wanted to call the wild lands along the Jordan River home, but John walked the dry rolling hills with ease. He didn't even mind when small lizards and scorpions scurried beneath the stones at his feet. At night he listened to the yipping of the foxes on the hunt and the call of the night owls. In the stillness of nature John thought about God. If he invited someone to dinner, they had better be prepared to be a little bugged because John dined on grasshoppers and wild bee honey.

Besides his unique lifestyle, what was so special about John? First off, he could sure preach a sermon about God and attract a crowd. *"All the people from the countryside of Judea went out to him. All the people from Jerusalem went too"* (Mark 1:5).

What exactly was John telling the curious that came out to see him? He was telling them to tell God they were sorry

for their sins. But that's not all. He told them to change their hearts and change their ways! And to celebrate his or her new life for God by being baptized in front of everybody.

From the water's edge he'd preach to the crowd sitting along the river. John would wade out into the Jordan River, letting the water swirl around his legs for hours. One by one the repentant watchers would slip down the dusty bank and wade into the cool water. Then he'd baptize them in the water. By doing this, they were showing that they were giving over their lives to what God wanted

them to do. He was helping people get clean inside and out. That's why they called him John the Baptist.

Naturally this unusual man attracted attention. Leaders and teachers came to question him. Who was he and why was he doing this? John answered, *"I'm the messenger who is calling out in the desert, 'Make the way for the Lord straight'"* *(John 1:23).*

John knew from babyhood that someone very special was coming who would change the world forever. He told everybody who would listen, *"After me, one will come who is more powerful than I am. I'm not good enough to bend down and untie his sandals. I baptize you with water. But he will baptize you with the Holy Spirit" (Mark 1:7–8).* John was God's way of letting everybody know that Jesus was here and that big things were about to happen!

One day John was preaching and baptizing people by the river when he looked to the shore. Who should be standing on the banks of the river? Jesus! John instantly knew who Jesus was. When Jesus asked to be baptized, John felt completely unworthy. After all, here was the Son of God asking to be baptized by him! *"But John tried to stop him. He told Jesus, 'I need to be baptized by you. So why do you come to me?'" (Matthew 3:14).*

Jesus understood John's feelings of uncertainty and reassured him. *"Let it be this way for now. It is right for us to do this. It carries out God's holy plan" (Matthew 3:15).* Jesus wanted to do everything according to His Father's will and to set an example for others by being baptized.

John agreed. So Jesus waded into the waters of the Jordan to stand beside him. John, no doubt with a racing heart and trembling hands, baptized Jesus. This must have been the most exciting moment of his life! So often John had preached of Jesus' coming, and now he stood beside

Him in the waters of the Jordan. But wait; that's not all! It gets even better!

"As soon as Jesus was baptized, he came up out of the water. At that moment heaven was opened. Jesus saw the Spirit of God coming down on him like a dove. A voice from heaven said, 'This is my Son, and I love him. I am very pleased with him'" (Matthew 3:16–17). God was also pleased with John; he had done the job God had given him to do. He introduced Jesus, God's only Son, to the world.

LET'S TALK:

God loves us and has made each of us unique and special. He's got an amazing life planned for us, and God will use our lives to help tell the world about His love. How do you think John felt about his life serving God?

The Meeting

No doubt Satan had been hanging around watching Jesus do His Father's work. And Satan was a tad uptight, upset, and really fed up about the whole thing. Jesus was a big problem for him. Jesus, after all, was here to take away our sins. Satan had to make a big move, but he was sly, and he was waiting for just the right moment to try to trip Jesus up. Could Satan lead Jesus astray like he had Adam and Eve?

After being baptized Jesus was led by the Holy Spirit into the desert to fast for forty days and forty nights. He didn't eat at all so that He could devote all His thoughts and energy to God. The desert was quiet and still, leaving

the hustle and bustle of the villages far away. Here, Jesus was free to worship God all day and all night. There were no interruptions. The hot days flowed into the cool nights, one upon the other. After those many days without food, Jesus was very hungry.

This, Satan must have thought, was the perfect time to catch Jesus a little off guard. Satan said to Him, *"If you are the Son of God, tell this stone to become bread" (Luke 4:3).* What a thing to say to a hungry person. And that's exactly why Satan said it.

Jesus answered right back with a Bible verse, *"It is written, 'Man doesn't live only on bread. He also lives on every word that comes from the mouth of God'" (Matthew 4:4).* Jesus trusted His Father and knew that being obedient was even more important than eating.

Clearly food wasn't a big enough temptation. Satan led Jesus up to a high place and showed Him in an instant all the mighty kingdoms of the entire world. Kingdoms with enormous armies, great lands, and castles filled with treasure. Satan said to Jesus, *"I will give you all their authority and glory. It has been given to me, and I can give it to anyone I want to. So if you worship me, it will all be yours" (Luke 4:6–7).* Well, this temptation was certainly a big leap from sandwich to super-ruler. Satan had increased the bait. Would Jesus bite?

Jesus answered, *"Get away from me, Satan! It is written, 'Worship the Lord your God. He is the only one you should serve'" (Matthew 4:10).*

"Ah," thought Satan, "why not use Bible verse to fight Bible verse." Satan took Jesus to Jerusalem to the highest point of the temple. What a view! The many buildings and gardens below made the city a patchwork of colors. The hills and valleys of the countryside faded into the misty horizon far across the desert. Satan continued his test because he wasn't giving up. He showed Jesus the dizzy heights and the roads and buildings far below. *"'If you are the Son God,' he said, 'throw yourself down from here. It is written, 'The Lord will command his angels to take good care of you. They will lift you up in their hands. Then you won't trip over a stone'"* (Luke 4:9–11).

Jesus quoted another Bible verse, *"Do not put the Lord your God to the test" (Luke 4:12)*. What a great answer! You don't have to test God to see if He loves you. He does!

Well, three strikes and Satan was out! Satan left and angels came down and took care of Jesus.

Jesus had passed Satan's tiresome temptation test without a mistake. Why? Every time Satan tried to tempt or trick Him, Jesus always choose to do things God's way.

When Eve was tempted, by the time that old slick operator was finished, Eve wasn't sure what God had really said. Satan had her all confused by his lies. But with Jesus it was a completely different story. Jesus knew His Father's heart and what the Bible tells us like the back of His hand. For each of Satan's tricks, Jesus knew and used God's words to both guide Him on what to do and stop Satan dead in his slippery tracks.

Satan couldn't throw God's plan off track but he would keep trying.

LET'S TALK:

Satan is still around today tempting us with all sorts of things. To avoid his traps, we have to do what Jesus did.

A) Love God.

B) Pray for help to avoid temptation.

C) Learn the Bible so that we know the truth.

D) Always choose to do things God's way.

With these four important points we can win the temptation struggle. It isn't easy, but with God's help we can do it. When you are tempted to do wrong things, what can you do to stay on the right godly path?

Follow the Leader

A gentle breeze cooled the heat of the day allowing people and animals to move from their shady resting spots into the bright sun. John the Baptist sat with two of his students discussing the Bible. Suddenly John stopped talking and stared at a man walking down the dusty road. He pointed to the man and turned to his disciples. *"Look! The Lamb of God!" (John 1:36).* The men watched as Jesus passed by.

John's students got up and followed Jesus. "Then Jesus turned around and saw them following. He asked, *'What do you want?' They said, 'Rabbi,* [which means Teacher] *where are you staying?'" (John 1:38).* Jesus invited them to join Him for the day and He talked with them. One of the men was named Andrew, and he was so excited about meeting Jesus that he ran to tell his brother, Simon. Simon was a fisherman, so perhaps Andrew found him repairing his nets or unloading fish from his boats. Andrew just blurted out, *"We have found the Messiah" (John 1:41).* Simon could tell Andrew was bursting with excitement, so he also wanted to meet Jesus.

The two men approached Jesus and an eager Andrew introduced his brother, Simon. *"Jesus looked at him and said,*

'You are Simon, son of John. You will be called Cephas"
[which, when translated is Peter] *(John 1:42)*. The
name Peter means "rock." Jesus knew that Simon Peter
had a special job to do.

Jesus traveled across the countryside teaching in the
many villages and towns. Everyone who heard His words
was amazed. Jesus had many wonderful things to teach
about His Father and about heaven. It was important
that what He taught be remembered and passed on
to others. To do this job, Jesus selected special
friends that would travel with Him and learn
from Him. He wanted twelve students or
disciples. One day Jesus was walking
along the Sea of Galilee (which is
actually a large lake) when he

spotted Peter, Andrew, and their father in a fishing boat casting their nets into the lake.

"'Come. Follow me,' Jesus said. 'I will make you fishers of people'" (Matthew 4:19). The two brothers left their father and followed Jesus! Jesus also called two more fishermen named James and John. And they also went with Him.

A tax collector named Matthew was busy at his tax booth in the village. Matthew collected taxes from his own people for the Romans, who ruled over the land where they lived. Tax collectors were not very popular. Jesus spotted Matthew in the crowded market and approached the booth. Every eye in the market was probably watching the young preacher. Why was He talking to that tax collector?

Matthew looked up and was shocked to see Jesus standing before him. He was even more shocked when the preacher asked Matthew to follow Him. The tax collector immediately got up, left his old life behind, and followed Jesus.

Over the days and weeks, many others joined Him as well. One day Jesus went out to a mountainside alone to pray all night. He was probably talking to God, His Father, about who the special twelve disciples should be. The next day He gathered the many men that had been following Him. No doubt each man was very nervous as they waited to see if their name would be called. They understood it wouldn't be an easy job being a disciple. It would mean hard work, and their lives would be changed forever. But still they hoped to hear their names called. *"Simon was one of them. Jesus gave him the named Peter. There were also Simon's brother Andrew, James, John, Philip and Bartholomew. And there were Matthew, Thomas, and James, son of Alphaeus. There were also Simon who was*

47

called the Zealot and Judas, son of James. Judas Iscariot was one of them too. He was the one who would later hand Jesus over to his enemies" (Luke 6:14–16). Peter and Andrew probably hugged each other, they were so happy!

The twelve men Jesus chose committed their lives to Him and put their futures in Jesus' hands. These men would teach others what Jesus taught them. They would carry Jesus' words to the world.

LET'S TALK:

The twelve disciples started out by choosing to follow Jesus. They could have stayed home but they didn't. Jesus saw their faithfulness and chose them for a very important job. Did you know Jesus has a very special job for you too?

When you chose to follow Jesus by living the way He wants you to, He will show you what your special job is. When Jesus calls your name, be ready to say, "Here I am!" Jesus will be your teacher and friend for life. Talk with your parents about your future with Jesus.

Open Door

"Jesus went all over Galilee. There he taught in the synagogues. He preached the good news of God's kingdom. He healed every illness and sickness the people had" *(Matthew 4:23).* Stories about this new teacher and His twelve disciples spread from village to town to city. There had never been anybody quite like Jesus before! People claimed He healed the sick, and His teachings were like none they had ever heard. Jesus was the talk of the nation. Everybody wanted to see this miracle worker. And everybody wondered why He had come? Everywhere Jesus went He was followed by hundreds of people.

One day Jesus sat on the side of a mountain, below Him

a crowd of hundreds dotted the countryside waiting to hear and see this amazing teacher and healer. Some had come carrying the sick hoping for a miracle, but others had come just to listen. Jesus began to teach the crowd. He started by saying, *"Blessed are those who are spiritually needy. The kingdom of heaven belongs to them"* (Matthew 5:3). The people fell silent. What was that? The poor get a kingdom? That got their attention.

Jesus continued, *"Blessed are those who are sad. They will be comforted. Blessed are those who are free of pride. They will be given the earth. Blessed are those who are hungry and thirsty for what is right. They will be filled. Blessed are those who show mercy. They will be shown mercy. Blessed are those whose hearts are pure. They will see God. Blessed are those who make peace. They will be called sons of God. Blessed are those who suffer for*

doing what is right. The kingdom of heaven belongs to them"
(Matthew 5:4–10).

Wait a minute! The people looked at each other. What was He saying? The crowd had never heard a sermon like this. There were rewards in heaven for ordinary people? The earth belonged to peacemakers and the weak...not kings and armies? The crowd murmured and stirred with excitement.

Jesus continued to tell them about His great and loving Father in heaven, and about the things that were really important: forgiving the wrongs of others, loving your enemy, giving to the needy, and not judging others. He taught that true treasure is doing what pleases God. He encouraged people to always do what was right. *"Let your light shine in front of others. Then they will see the good things you do. And they will praise your Father who is in heaven"*

(Matthew 5:16). Jesus told them of His Father's love for them. He explained how God wanted to hear each of their prayers and, like a loving Father, would answer them.

Then He taught them how to pray. *"When you pray, go into your room. Close the door and pray to your Father, who can't be seen. He will reward you. Your Father sees what is done secretly"* (Matthew 6:6). Did that mean they could pray to God anywhere and anytime? Jesus explained that praying was really talking honestly to God, not something you do to impress people. Praying to your God should be simple because He already knows what you need before you even ask.

Jesus taught, *"Ask, and it will be given to you. Search, and you will find. Knock, and the door will be opened to you. Everyone who asks will receive. He who searches will find. The door will be opened to the one who knocks"* (Matthew 7:7–8). The crowd was amazed at the things He taught! It seemed so simple but also so right!

Jesus helped the crowd and His disciples to understand how important each and every person was to God. *"Look at the birds of the air. They don't plant or gather crops. They don't put away crops in storerooms. But your Father who is in heaven feeds them. Aren't you worth much more than they are?"* (Matthew 6:26). His message was clear—talk with God through prayer because your heavenly Father wants to hear from you. Be a light to the world by doing things God's way, and don't worry because God will take care of you!

The crowd was awed and inspired by this new picture of God. But it wasn't only what Jesus said and the miracles He did. It was clear He knew about the things He taught! This teacher was clearly special because He was full of God's love and mercy.

LET'S TALK:

When Jesus taught, He made things simple. He taught that prayer was very important but it should also be very easy. God loves you and He wants you to talk to Him just like you would talk to a close friend. Simple! Talk to God anytime, anywhere, and about anything. God's listening and wants to get in there and work in your life. Would you like to talk with God right now? Your mom and dad or even your grandparent can help you with your prayer. All you have to do is ask!

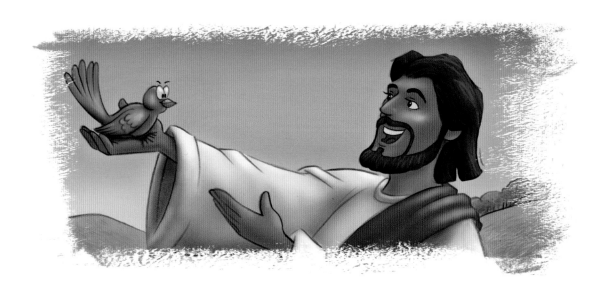

Tell Us a Story!

People really haven't changed that much over thousands of years. Everybody loves a great story! Even in Jesus' time, folks would sit around in the evening and listen to a good story told well. Jesus used this love of adventure or surprise to help Him explain what heaven and God were like. When Jesus answered questions, or had something really important to say, He often told a story. These tales are called parables.

One day, Peter sat deep in thought with a puzzled look across his face. Finally he got up and looked for his teacher. *"Peter came to Jesus. He asked, 'Lord, how many times should I forgive my brother when he sins against me? Up to seven times?'*

Jesus answered, 'I tell you, not seven times, but 77 times'" (Matthew 18:21–22). Then He told this story to help Peter and others listening to understand His answer.

A kind king decided that it was time to talk with each of his servants about how much they owed and if they could pay him back. *"A man who owed him millions of dollars was brought to him" (Matthew 18:24)*. A big, big debt of millions of dollars spelled trouble.

Jesus knew that everybody in the crowd understood the fear of getting in debt and going to prison. People could relate to His story ,and so they listened carefully.

As it turned out, this man couldn't repay the king. The king was understandably very upset and commanded *"the man, his wife, his children, and all he owned had to be sold to pay back what he owed" (Matthew 18:25)*.

The man instantly fell on his knees before the king. *"'Give me time,' he begged. 'I'll pay everything back'" (Matthew 18:26)*. The king wasn't a bad fellow, and *"his master felt sorry for him. He forgave him what he owed and let him go" (Matthew 18:27)*. What a truly kind, forgiving, and generous king! The man was free of his huge debt and his family was safe! He probably left the throne room clicking his heels very thankful and happy.

Jesus' listeners were so pleased. They loved happy endings! But wait, the story doesn't end there. Jesus continued with His tale. *"But then that servant went out and found one of the other servants who owed him a few dollars. He grabbed him and began to choke him. 'Pay back what you owe me!' he said. The other servant fell on his knees. 'Give me time,' he begged him. 'I'll pay you back'" (Matthew 18:28–29)*.

The people were all ears as Jesus continued. *"But the first servant refused. Instead, he went and had the man thrown into prison. The man would be held there until he could pay back*

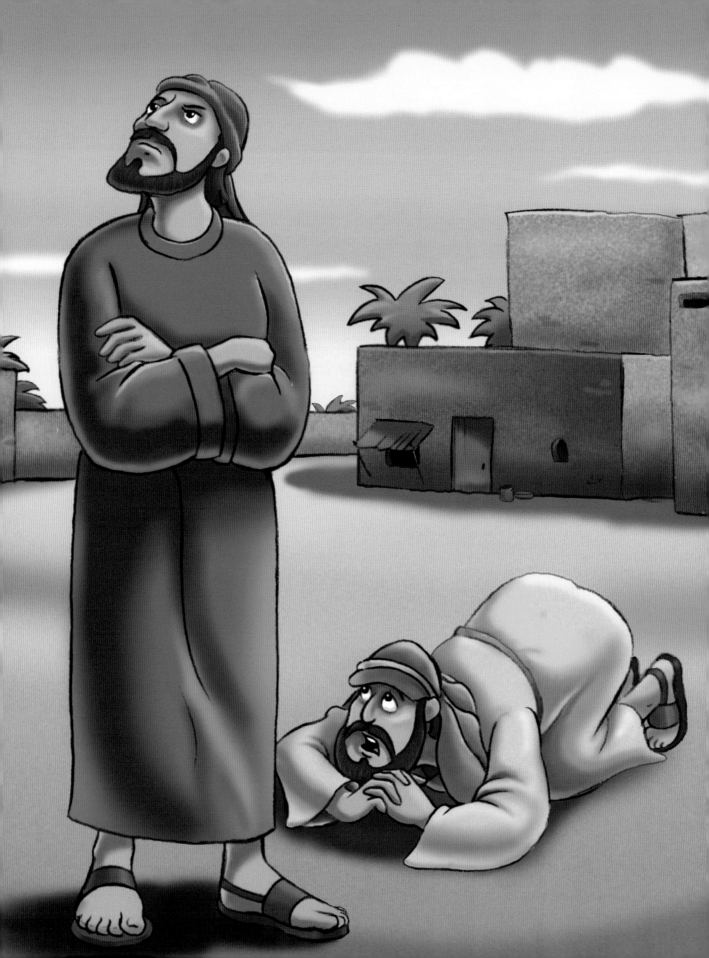

what he owed" (Matthew 18:30).

Jesus' audience was shocked at this twist in the story. How could this man actually refuse to forgive the other man's debt? *"The other servants saw what had happened. It troubled them greatly. They went and told their master everything that had happened" (Matthew 18:31).* The king listened and then asked for the man to be sent to him.

To the audience's delight, Jesus told how the unforgiving servant was brought back to the king. The king was very angry, *"'You evil servant,' he said. 'I forgave all that you owed me because you begged me to. Shouldn't you have had mercy on the other servant just as I had mercy on you?'" (Matthew 18:32–33).* The king changed his earlier decision. Instead he demanded full payment of the man's debt and promptly turned the unforgiving servant over to the jailers until he could pay back all that he owed.

The crowd was very pleased with the outcome of the story! The unforgiving man clearly deserved all that he got.

But, Jesus ended this parable with this warning, *"This is how my Father in heaven will treat each of you unless you forgive your brother from your heart" (Matthew 18:35).* The crowd may have fallen silent as each thought about their own lives and their own treatment of others.

Jesus told the story so the people would understand how kind and forgiving God was to them. God was like the kind king! But it was also a warning. If you want to be forgiven by your heavenly Father, then forgiving others should be your first order of the day.

After telling a parable, Jesus would often explain the meaning so everybody understood His heavenly lessons well. Jesus always used the perfect story to teach the right lesson at exactly the right moment.

LET'S TALK:

Jesus told this story so we would always remember to be kind and generous with everyone, just like God is with us. Forgiving others shouldn't be a sometime thing; it should be an all the time thing. What kind of changes in our lives can we make so what we do and how we treat others is more like Jesus? Remember God forgives us as soon as we ask!

Healing-A Lifetime Gift

One day Jesus took a boat to the other side of a lake. By the time He reached the opposite shore, a crowd already waited for Him because they had heard about His miracles and teaching. A cheer went up as the boat reached the bank. It rocked as some of the people rushed into the water to touch Jesus first. The disciples helped clear a path as Jesus walked onto the beach into the waiting gathering.

A very worried man named Jairus pushed through the people and fell at Jesus' feet pleading, *"Please come. My little daughter is dying. Place your hands on her to heal her. Then she will live" (Mark 5:23).* So Jesus went with the worried father.

Many people in the crowd knew Jairus because he was an important leader at the synagogue. They followed so closely that it was hard for Jesus and Jairus to press forward down the road. People were pushing and shoving all trying to get close to Jesus. No doubt the disciples were also trying to stay close to their teacher to protect Him from the eager crowd.

Now, in this crowd was a woman who had been very sick for twelve long years. *"She had suffered a great deal, even though she had gone to many doctors. She had spent all the money she had. But she was getting worse, not better"* (Mark 5:26). The poor woman had used all her strength to find Jesus, but to her dismay she was one of hundreds who pushed and shoved to meet Him. Pressed between so many bodies she must have felt faint and weak. Jesus was her last hope of getting well and she was determined to get close to Him. *"She came up behind him in the crowd and touched his clothes. She thought, 'I just need to touch his clothes. Then I will be healed'"* (Mark 5:27–28).

Instantly the woman felt different. Suddenly she realized she didn't feel weak anymore! Her whole body was free of sickness! It had been so long since she had felt well! She cried because she was so happy!

"At once Jesus knew that power had gone out from him. He turned around in the crowd. He asked, 'Who touched my clothes?'" (Mark 5:30).

Some of the disciples were beside Jesus in the midst of all the jostling people. As far as they could tell, any one of a hundred pushing and shoving people could have touched their teacher.

"But Jesus kept looking around. He wanted to see who had touched him. Then the woman came and fell at his feet. She knew what had happened to her. She was shaking with fear. But

she told him the whole truth" (Mark 5:32–33).

Jesus was filled with loving care for her and He said, "Dear woman, your faith has healed you. Go in peace. You are free from your suffering" (Mark 5:34).

While Jesus was speaking with the woman, some men pushed into the crowd to find Jairus. "'Your daughter is dead,' they said. 'Why bother the teacher anymore?'" (Mark 5:35). The poor father must have trembled as he heard this terrible news. His heart was breaking. But Jesus ignored the men and spoke directly to Jairus, "Don't be afraid. Just believe" (Mark 5:36).

Jesus set out for Jairus' house allowing Peter, James, and John, the brother of James, to go with them. Even before they came to the house they could hear the wailing and crying of the little girl's family and friends. Jesus entered the home and spoke to the grieving family, "Why all this confusion and sobbing? The child is not dead. She is only sleeping" (Mark 5:39). They did not believe Him. It was clear to everyone the child was dead.

Jesus sent them out of the house and asked the parents and His disciples to join Him. Jesus went over to the little child and took her gently by the hand. He said, "'Talitha koum!' This means, 'Little girl, I say to you, get up!'" (Mark 5:41). Jairus could not believe what he saw. Immediately his precious little girl stood up and walked around. The family hugged her with tears of thanksgiving in their eyes. This was truly a miracle. Jesus gave them strict orders not to tell anyone and then told them to give their daughter some food and to take care of her. Jesus entered a home full of great sadness and left it full of happiness and thanksgiving!

Jesus was full of love and compassion. What better way was there to teach of God's love than by healing people of their hurts? That's a lesson in love.

LET'S TALK:

Jesus wanted us to know how much God loves us. Our heavenly Father wants to care for us! Miracles still happen even today. Some happen quickly while others may take years. Just know that Jesus loves you and wants to help you have a good life. Can you think of some people you'd like to pray for? Your prayers are important!

Making Miracles

ots of children excitedly followed the crowd who went to see the teacher everyone was talking about. They scrambled up trees, hills, and boulders to see Jesus' boat come ashore. The children watched wide-eyed as Jesus did miracles. Suddenly the blind could see; the crippled could walk; and the sick danced laughing and thanking God because they had been healed.

One boy stood among the crowd watching with growing excitement. Even though the sun dipped lower in the sky, he wasn't ready to go home. What if something important happened?

The disciples realized the crowd wasn't leaving and

asked Jesus to send them away because there was no food. *"Jesus replied, 'They don't need to go away. You give them something to eat'" (Matthew 14:16).*

Poor Philip did a quick headcount and realized there were thousands and thousands of people. *"Philip answered him, 'Eight months' pay would not buy enough bread for each one to have a bite!'" (John 6:7).* To his surprise Jesus didn't seem the least bit worried.

The curious boy squeezed past people and dodged under legs until he sat near the front. In a leather bag he carried his lunch.

The disciples scratched their heads over what should be done. *"Another of his disciples spoke up. It was Andrew, Simon Peter's brother. He said, 'Here is a boy with five small loaves of barley bread. He also has two small fish. But how far will that go in such a large crowd?'" (John 6:8–9).*

Now, you didn't have to be a math genius to figure out that this boy-sized lunch wasn't going to go too far. But, faith has a way making the impossible possible.

"Jesus said, 'Have the people sit down.' There was plenty of grass in that place, and they sat down. The number of men among them was about 5,000. Then Jesus took the loaves and gave thanks. He handed out the bread to those who were seated. He gave them as much as they wanted. And he did the same with the fish" (John 6:10–11).

Jesus' disciples just kept handing out fish and bread until everybody in that crowd got more than enough to eat! There wasn't a guest at this incredible banquet who wasn't surprised and amazed! Everybody, that is, except Jesus.

"When all of them had enough to eat, Jesus spoke to his disciples. 'Gather the leftover pieces,' he said. 'Don't waste anything.' So they gathered what was left over from the five barley loaves. They filled 12 baskets with the pieces left by

those who had eaten"(John 6:12–13). Wow they had left-overs! What a meal!

Later, Jesus sent His disciples across the lake in the boat while He said goodbye to the crowd. Then when He was alone, He prayed. That evening the disciples were in the middle of the lake when a strong wind whipped up the

waves, making the small
boat pitch and turn. The men
clung to anything in the boat, frightened
they may be washed overboard and drowned.
One disciple stared out into the storm. He thought
he saw something out on the rolling waves in the growing
dark. What was it? Then all the men saw, but they couldn't
believe their eyes. There was their teacher walking calmly
across the storm tossed water. *"'It's a ghost!' they said. And
they cried out in fear. Right away Jesus called out to them, 'Be
brave! It is I. Don't be afraid.' 'Lord, is it you?' Peter asked. 'If it
is, tell me to come to you on the water.' 'Come,' Jesus said"
(Matthew 14:26–29).*

   Peter probably took a deep breath as he swung his legs
over the side of the boat. The waves were heavy but he

trusted Jesus! He put both feet on the water and stood. Peter with confident steps began to walk towards Jesus. But as he got farther from the boat, Peter glanced down at the dark wild waves just beneath his feet. His faith started to drop, and so did he. As Peter began to sink, he cried out, *"Lord! Save me!" (Matthew 14:30).*

Immediately Jesus reached out and caught hold of Peter. *"'Your faith is so small!' he said. 'Why did you doubt me?'" (Matthew 14:31).* Jesus helped Peter back in the boat. The other disciples were completely amazed for the second time in one day. Jesus was truly the Son of God!

LET'S TALK:

Jesus did many miraculous things, and like a collection of beautiful pictures, each miracle shows us in different ways how wonderful God is. God takes care of us each and everyday. He has given us absolutely everything we have from the clothes we wear to the house we live in. They all make our lives better. Think about some of the things God has given us that make our lives better!

No Trouble at All

People talked about Jesus around the water well in many of the villages. As women gathered to fetch water, wash clothes, or tend to children, they repeated amazing stories of this miracle worker from Nazareth. Some had heard of His teaching. Others talked with people who had been healed by Him. Their village was a buzz with the news that Jesus was nearby teaching on the banks of the Jordan River. Some of the mothers gathered up their children and headed out to find Him. The women chatted together while their children skipped ahead of them along the dusty road.

It wasn't long before the women spotted a huge crowd

along the muddy river. The sick and needy were all around Jesus, hoping to touch Him, or be touched by Him. His faithful disciples made sure the people gave their teacher room to move and work. On that day the crowd was particularly large because many wanted to be healed. Part of this crowd was a group called the Pharisees. They were religious leaders. They frowned and brooded as they watched. Why was everybody so interested in this fellow from Nazareth? They wanted to prove to the people Jesus wasn't really that special by trying to trick Him with difficult questions. But Jesus always had just the right answer.

The mothers and children had joined the large gathering and had made their way to the front of the crowd to see

Him. They listened to Jesus and the Pharisees talk. It was clear to them that Jesus was no ordinary preacher because He truly seemed to have the love and wisdom of God.

The women waited and hoped that perhaps during a small break in the day's busy work Jesus would have time to

bless their children. Finally being bold, they pushed their little ones forward to have Jesus place His hands on them and pray for them.

"But the disciples told the people to stop" (Matthew 19:13). Didn't these women know that Jesus was a busy man? And today of all days! With the important Pharisees hanging around asking tricky questions, Jesus certainly didn't need to be bothered by crying babies. The disciples began to shoo the children and mothers away.

Jesus saw what was happening and called out, *"Let the little children come to me. Don't keep them away"* (Matthew 19:14).

Jesus' smiled as He motioned for the children to come to Him. The children trusted Him and flocked to His side.

How amazing! Jesus dropped everything He was doing just to spend some time with children. The Pharisees probably watched in surprise and so did the sheepish disciples. Looking at the men gathered around Him and back at the beautiful children in front of Him, Jesus said, *"The kingdom of heaven belongs to people like them"* (Matthew 19:14).

No doubt the mothers gave the disciples a "look" and then smiled with pride. It was clear to them that Jesus loved their little ones as much as they did. Jesus was indeed very special! Then they watched as He placed His hands on each little child and prayed for them.

Jesus loved and admired the simple trusting faith of a child. The disciples came to Jesus and asked, *"Who is the most important person in the kingdom of heaven?"* (Matthew 18:1).

Jesus called to a child nearby and motioned for him to stand beside Him. The child instantly got up and stood beside Him. *"Jesus said, 'What I'm about to tell you is true. You need to change and become like little children. If you*

don't, you will never enter the kingdom of heaven. Anyone who becomes as free of pride as this child is the most important in the kingdom of heaven. Anyone who welcomes a little child like this in my name welcomes me'" (Matthew 18:3–5). The religious leaders standing there probably figured that they'd be first in line for the best spots in heaven because they knew the Bible and always acted very holy. But God loves us all! Jesus pointed to the children because He knew they simply loved God.

LET'S TALK:

God sent His Son, Jesus, into this world for everyone, not just adults. God loves you as much as He loves anyone else, and you are just as important to Him now as you will be when you're all grown-up. Remember next time you pray to thank God for loving you so much. Don't forget He's always listening!

Last Supper

t was spring and the Passover Feast was quickly approaching. Remember the Passover was a special holiday to celebrate God bringing Moses and His people out of Egypt. Perhaps Jesus and the disciples were in the country sitting in the shade of an olive orchard discussing the Scriptures. The afternoon was lazy, and they could hear a young boy herding noisy geese along the road and women slapping wet clothes against river rocks to get them clean. Life was peaceful and full of good things.

The disciples asked Jesus where He'd like to hold their Passover meal. They had to find a place to prepare a banquet table and roast a lamb for the feast. Jesus instructed Peter and John to find a certain homeowner who would have a large upper room ready and waiting for them. The disciples rushed to do as they were told.

When everything was ready, Jesus joined His twelve disciples at the table. But this was no ordinary Passover feast! Jesus knew that this would be His last special time with His friends before He died.

Jesus wanted to show His disciples how much He loved them. Before the meal was served, He poured water in a bowl and began to wash and dry each of His dear friend's feet. The disciples were deeply touched because usually a servant is the one who washes his master's feet.

Jesus explained, *"I, your Lord and Teacher, have washed your feet. So you also should wash one another's feet. I have given you an example. You should do as I have done for you. What I'm about to tell you is true. A servant is not more important than his master. And a messenger is not more important than the one who sends him. Now you know these things. So you will be blessed if you do them" (John 13:14–17).* Jesus, God's only Son, had come to serve.

The disciples ate well and enjoyed the relaxing time together! Finally Jesus told them what was going to happen, *"I have really looked forward to eating this Passover meal with you. I wanted to do this before I suffer" (Luke 22:15).* He told them how very soon He would be taken away from them and be put to death. The happy table must have fallen very quiet and still. The disciples loved Jesus and did not want Him to be hurt in any way and did not want Him to leave them either.

Jesus took the special Passover bread and drink and gave thanks to God. He passed them to His friends. When each man had received his share, Jesus asked them to remember

81

the things He said and did every time they broke bread together and drank from the cup. This was the first Communion ever!

The Passover meal celebrated God's rescue of Moses and His people from Egypt. Now when we take communion we remember how God sent His Son, Jesus, to free us from sin. To do this miracle Jesus already knew that He must die. He faced His death with a peace that comes from knowing that this was all part of God's plan. Jesus' friends were very distressed, but there was more shocking news.

Jesus told the disciples that one of them would help the

Pharisees and other leaders who wanted to arrest Him. A friend would help the soldiers arrest Him. The men were very sad, and each wondered which of them would do such a thing? But Jesus already knew who.

Jesus said to Judas Iscariot, *"Do quickly what you are going to do"* (John 13:27). Judas left the supper to have Jesus arrested.

Peter was greatly concerned, and he said, *"Lord, I am ready to go with you to prison and to death"* (Luke 22:33).

Jesus looked into Peter's worried face and was saddened because He knew troubled times were coming for Peter. He also knew His friend would feel so lost and frightened that he'd actually pretend not to be one of the disciples. Jesus

told His good friend, *"Will you really give your life for me? What I'm about to tell you is true. Before the rooster crows, you will say three times that you don't know me!"* (John 13:38). Peter and the others were very upset.

Jesus reassured them, *"Do not let your hearts be troubled. Trust in God. Trust in me also. There are many rooms in my Father's house. If this were not true, I would have told you. I am going there to prepare a place for you. If I go and do that, I will come back. And I will take you to be with me. Then you will also be where I am. You know the way to the place where I am going"* (John 14:1–4).

The disciples didn't understand this until later. But Jesus was letting them know that He had to die so that all of us could be with Him and His Father in heaven forever.

LET'S TALK:

When you become part of God's family, Jesus makes a special place just for you in God's house in heaven. What kind of a special place do you think Jesus has for you? What kinds of things did Jesus say about heaven? You can find the answer in the Bible!

Troubled Times

Jesus and His disciples went to a garden called Gethsemane to pray. Jesus was very sad. *"Then he fell with his face to the ground. He prayed, 'My Father, if it is possible, take this cup of suffering away from me. But let what you want to be done, not what I want'"* (Matthew 26:39).

Then from the nighttime shadows Judas appeared and gave Jesus a kiss on the cheek. It was meant as sign to the waiting soldiers. Jesus asked, *"Judas, are you handing over the Son of Man with a kiss?" (Luke 22:48).*

The soldiers rushed in to arrest Jesus. But the disciples tried to protect Him. Men pushed and shoved in the light of

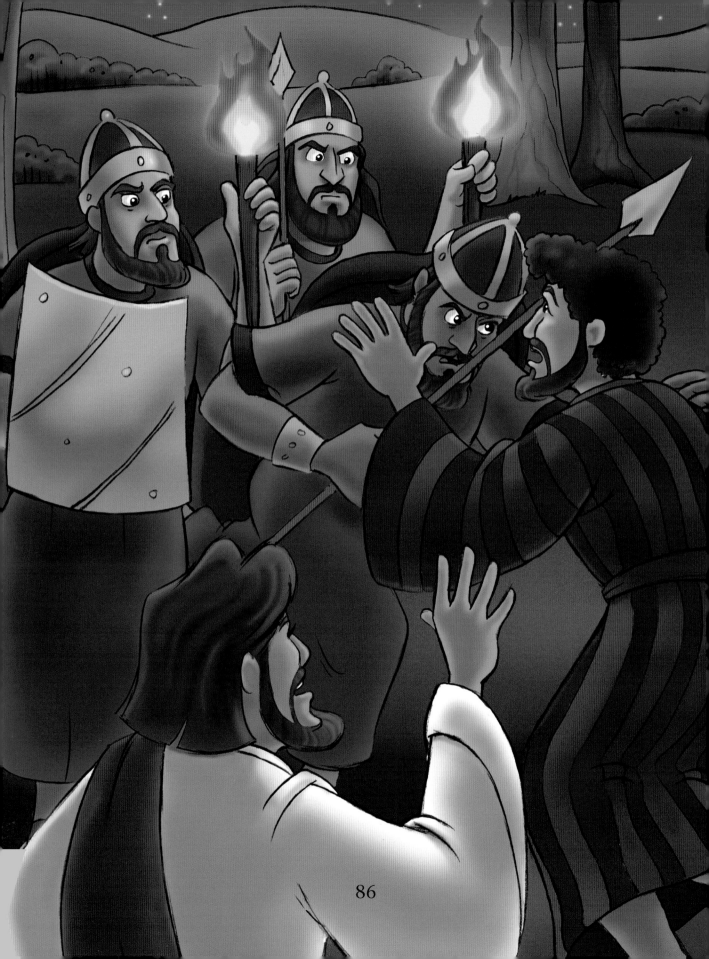

the flickering torches. A man cried out in pain and surprise. Jesus quickly stopped the fighting and told His disciples to put away their swords. A servant for the priests held his head in pain. Jesus walked up to the unhappy man and touched him. Instantly the servant was healed.

Jesus went quietly away with the soldiers. The disciples ran into the night, afraid that they, too, would be arrested. But Peter followed and saw they had taken Jesus to the high priest's house.

It was cold and Peter huddled around a fire outside the house to wait. Everyone was talking excitedly about Jesus' arrest. A servant girl pointed at Peter in the firelight. *"This man was with Jesus" (Luke 22:56)*.

Peter pulled his cloak tight around his face and shook his head, *"Woman, I don't know him" (Luke 22:57)*. Peter was frightened that they may also arrest him. Two more times Peter claimed not to know Jesus. Suddenly his teacher's words came back to him. It was true! He had disowned Jesus three times! Filled with great guilt and shame, Peter ran away crying.

Jesus was brought before the religious leaders. Caiaphas, the head priest stared at Jesus. Around him sat all the teachers of the law and all the elders of the temple. Caiaphas had gathered them to hear all kinds of made-up lies about Jesus. He wanted this dangerous troublemaker put to death. But all Caiaphas' plans and lies still weren't enough to find Jesus guilty. When questioned, Jesus remained silent and would not answer them.

Then Caiaphas said, *"I command you under oath by the living God. Tell us if you are the Christ, the Son of God" (Matthew 26:63)*.

Jesus had to answer this question. *"'Yes. It is just as you say,' Jesus replied" (Matthew 26:64)*. Then Jesus began to preach to them.

This got the unbelieving Caiaphas so upset that he ripped his clothes. *"He has spoken a very evil thing against God!" (Matthew 26:65).* Caiaphas thought Jesus was saying things that were hurtful to God. He just couldn't see the truth.

They all wanted to put Jesus to death for saying He was the Son of God. So they took Him to the Roman ruler Pilate to get permission. Pilate listened to the angry men and talked to Jesus himself. But he could find no reason to kill Jesus.

So Pilate had Jesus whipped instead. The Roman soldiers hit Jesus and laughed at Him for saying He was a king. They put a purple robe on Him and a crown of long twisted thorn branches. But this was still not enough for the religious leaders.

Jesus stood before Pilate again. The Roman ruler asked Jesus many questions, but Jesus said nothing. *"'Do you refuse to speak to me?' Pilate said. 'Don't you understand? I have the power to set you free or to nail you to a cross.' Jesus answered, 'You were given power from heaven. If you weren't, you would have no power over me'" (John 19:10–11).* Jesus understood that this was all part of His Father's plan.

Pilate was surprised and troubled by Jesus' answer. He tried to set Jesus free. But the religious leaders got so very upset that they almost caused a riot. An angry mob gathered shouting and pointing at Jesus, *"Kill him! Kill him! Crucify him!" (John 19:15).*

Pilate wanted to keep the peace so he ordered Jesus to be put to death. But first he ordered a bowl of water be brought to him. A servant quickly held the bowl in front of Pilate. The Roman held out his hands for all to see and then washed them in front of the angry crowd. *"'I am not*

guilty of this man's death,' he said. 'You are accountable for that!'" (Matthew 27:24). Jesus had done nothing wrong and had only spoken the truth. But He was ordered to be put to death.

LET'S TALK:
It must have been very sad for the disciples to see Jesus arrested and mistreated. Sometimes things happen and we don't understand why. We should always talk to God about everything and trust Him no matter what. What should you do when sad things happen in your life? Can God help? Can you name some ways God helps us?

The End?

Everybody in the city had heard that the teacher from Nazareth had been arrested and now was going to be killed. They gathered along the street to catch a glimpse of Him as He was taken out of the city to be put to death. Among the crowd were the disciples and others that knew and loved Jesus. Their hearts were breaking with sadness. This was the day Jesus had warned them would come.

The Roman soldiers gathered the prisoners. They placed a large wooden cross on Jesus' back so He could carry it out of the city to the spot where He would die. The cross was heavy as Jesus carried it into the streets. Each jolt of the

cross as it dragged against the rough streets made Jesus even weaker. One soldier waited impatiently as Jesus struggled with His burden. The soldier searched the crowd and grabbed a man named Simon. Calling another soldier to help, he put Jesus' cross on Simon's back and ordered him to carry it. The sad march continued and a crowd of people followed behind crying loudly.

When they got to the spot called "the Skull," the soldiers took Jesus and put Him on the cross and raised it up. Two criminals were also being executed with Jesus on either side of Him.

One criminal said to Jesus, *"Aren't you the Christ? Save yourself! Save us!" (Luke 23:39).*

But the other man scolded him. *"'Don't you have any respect for God,' he said. 'Remember, you are under the same sentence of death. We are being punished fairly. We are getting just what our actions call for. But this man hasn't done anything wrong.' Then he said, 'Jesus, remember me when you come into your kingdom.' Jesus answered him, 'What I'm about to tell you is true. Today you will be with me in paradise'" (Luke 23:40–43).*

Even then the soldiers and some of the religious leaders still made fun of Jesus. Some shouted, *"He saved others. Let him save himself if he is the Christ of God, the Chosen One" (Luke 23:35).*

Jesus was filled with great sadness and pity for these men and asked His Father in heaven something very special. *"Father, forgive them. They don't know what they are doing" (Luke 23:34).* Jesus' love for all people still included the ones that were hurting Him.

Jesus became weaker. The crowd gasped as the sun just suddenly stopped shining. A strange darkness had come over the land, and day was now like night for three hours. It seemed all of earth cried for the Son of the Creator.

Jesus sighed in His pain, *"It is finished"* *(John 19:30)*. And He called out in a loud voice, *"Father, into your hands I commit my very life"* *(Luke 23:46)*. Then Jesus took His last breath and died. He had truly done all the work God had sent Him to do.

Standing near the cross was a Roman centurion or captain. He was a tough man with a hundred soldiers under his command. He had seen many men die both in battle and crucified like Jesus. The centurion had noted everything that had happened and said, *"Jesus was surely a man who did what was right"* *(Luke 23:47)*. He ordered his soldiers to make sure Jesus was dead. They reported back that He was.

Silent crowds went back to their homes in the strange darkness and wondered what it all meant. Jesus' friends and believers wept while watching from a distance. They knew that the Son of God has just died. Jesus had been an innocent man. He had taken all the past, present, and future sins on Himself, and had allowed Himself to die for them. By doing this, He had

removed Adam and Eve's sin from us and had defeated all of Satan's plans.

Nicodemus and another believer named Joseph of Arimathea asked Pilate if they could have Jesus' body. Pilate with a wave of his hand agreed.

The two men took Jesus from the cross and carried Him away. Lovingly they prepared His body for burial by wrapping it with special spices and cloth. They took Jesus' body and laid it in a nearby garden in a new tomb or stone chamber cut in the side of a cliff. The tomb was a generous gift from Joseph of Arimathea. The people who loved Jesus reluctantly left Him in the tomb. But is that the end?

LET'S TALK:

Ever since Adam and Eve disobeyed God and were sent out of the garden, sin has kept us separated from God. But when Jesus died, He took the punishment for our sins Himself so that we could be God's children again. What kind of things can you do everyday to thank Jesus for all the things He has done for us?

He Is Alive!

The religious leaders thought the troublemaker named Jesus was gone for good. But still the high priests and Pharisees worried. You see, Jesus had said He would rise again after three days of being in the tomb. So the leaders sent soldiers to guard Jesus' tomb just in case those tricky disciples tried to steal the body and then tell everybody that Jesus rose from the dead.

The bored soldiers kept watch in the quiet garden. There wasn't much action in guarding a tomb. But this would be no ordinary day!

"There was a powerful earthquake. An angel of the Lord came down from heaven. The angel went to the tomb. He rolled back the stone and sat on it. His body shone like lightning. His

clothes were as white as snow" (Matthew 28:2–3). The guards took one look at this amazing heavenly being and every inch of their bodies began to shake with fear! They became like "dead men" (Matthew 28:4).

At that very moment a small group of women came to visit the tomb. The women blinked in surprise as they saw the beautiful angel and the frightened guards!

The angel spoke, "Don't be afraid. I know that you are looking for Jesus, who was crucified. He is not here! He has risen, just as he said he would! Come and see the place where he was lying. Go quickly! Tell his disciples, 'He has risen from the dead. He is going ahead of you into Galilee. There you will see him.' Now I have told you" (Matthew 28:5–7). The women hurried from the tomb filled with joy.

Meanwhile the guards' eyes fluttered slowly as they

looked around, but the angel was gone! With knocking knees they crept to the open tomb and peered inside. OH NO! Jesus' body was gone! The guards raced back to the city to tell the high priests.

After hearing the soldiers' report, the worried priests must have worn a hole in that floor pacing. What were they going to do now? People must never know the truth. They gave the guards a large sum of money telling them,

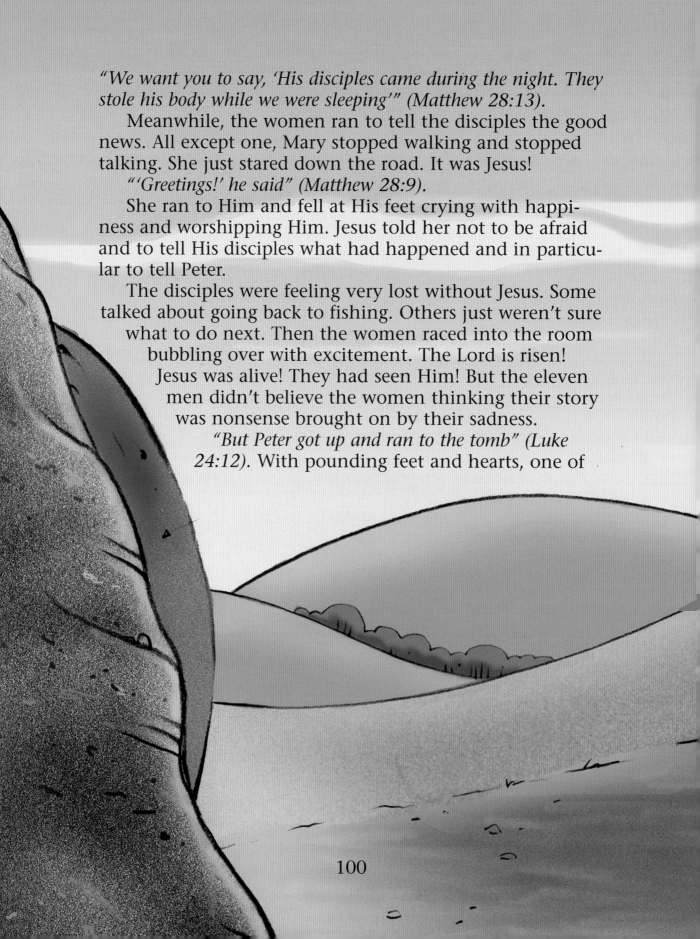

"We want you to say, 'His disciples came during the night. They stole his body while we were sleeping'" (Matthew 28:13).

Meanwhile, the women ran to tell the disciples the good news. All except one, Mary stopped walking and stopped talking. She just stared down the road. It was Jesus!

"'Greetings!' he said" (Matthew 28:9).

She ran to Him and fell at His feet crying with happiness and worshipping Him. Jesus told her not to be afraid and to tell His disciples what had happened and in particular to tell Peter.

The disciples were feeling very lost without Jesus. Some talked about going back to fishing. Others just weren't sure what to do next. Then the women raced into the room bubbling over with excitement. The Lord is risen! Jesus was alive! They had seen Him! But the eleven men didn't believe the women thinking their story was nonsense brought on by their sadness.

"But Peter got up and ran to the tomb" (Luke 24:12). With pounding feet and hearts, one of the other disciples outran Peter.

Peter reached the tomb and entered not knowing what he would find. *"He bent over and saw the strips of linen lying by themselves. Then he went away, wondering what had happened"* *(Luke 24:12).* Jesus was gone!

In the evening the disciples gathered together behind locked doors. The night owls screeched and the wind whistled through the olive trees, and each man listened to each little noise outside. What was that? Was it the temple soldiers already? With Jesus' body gone they expected to be blamed and arrested by the high priests.

Suddenly, and nobody was sure how or when, Jesus stood among them in the room. The disciples

leapt to their feet! They thought they had lost Jesus forever, but now amazingly He was here with them. He truly had risen from the dead!

Jesus greeted them. *"'May peace be with you!' Then he showed them his hands and his side" (John 20:20).* Jesus talked with them and the room was filled with His love!

But, Peter was still guilt ridden. The others gathered around Jesus but Peter held back quiet and uncertain. Could…would Jesus still love him after all that he had done? Jesus saw the troubled expression on His dear friend's face and knew what was troubling Peter.

Later, Jesus would talk with Peter letting him know He still loved him and still wanted him as a disciple. Peter was filled with relief because Jesus loved him no matter what!

LET'S TALK:

At Easter we celebrate Jesus being raised from the dead. Jesus is alive and He will be forever! And remember Jesus is always with us. There will always be times when we feel like we have disappointed Jesus. Times when we may not have done the right thing or treated people the way Jesus would have. What can we do to get right with Jesus? What did we learn from Peter's story?

Return

Over the next 40 days, the risen Jesus met the disciples many more times. He ate meals with them and talked with them. He explained the great event that had happened and what it all meant. Jesus even appeared to over 500 people at one time!

Jesus sat with his 11 disciples on a mountainside in Galilee. He studied these 11 good men and was very proud of them. He had a very important job for them to do. *"All authority in heaven and on earth has been given to me. So you must go and make disciples of all nations. Baptize them in the name of the Father and of the Son and of the Holy Spirit. Teach them to obey everything I have commanded you. And*

you can be sure that I am always with you, to the very end" (Matthew 28:18–19).

On the last day before Jesus left to go and join His Father in heaven again: *"'Do not leave Jerusalem,' he said. 'Wait for the gift my Father promised. You have heard me talk about it. John baptized with water. But in a few days you will be baptized with the Holy Spirit'"* (Acts 1:4–5). He explained the Holy Spirit would help them to tell the entire world about God's Word and the good news of His forgiveness through His Son!

Then before their eyes He rose up into the sky to heaven. The amazed disciples watched until a cloud hid Him from their view. Suddenly two men dressed in white stood beside them. *"'Men of Galilee,' they said, 'why do you stand here looking into the sky? Jesus has been taken away from you into heaven. But he will come back in the same way you saw him go'"* (Act 1:11).

There were more believers joining the disciples each day to learn about Jesus. By now there were 120 followers of Jesus. Just as Jesus had instructed, His disciples were spreading the good news!

Being obedient to Jesus' orders, the disciples stayed in the city of Jerusalem waiting for God's gift. The disciples were together in one room when suddenly the quiet room was shaken with the roaring rush of an incredibly strong wind which filled the entire house. *"They saw something that looked like tongues of fire. The flames separated and settled on each of them"* (Act 2:3). Then each person was filled with God's gift of the Holy Spirit. The Holy Spirit would give them power and boldness to tell people about Jesus. No matter where the disciples went to preach, God's gift would be there to assist them. It would help them find the right words, miracles, and courage to tell everybody, friend or enemy, about Jesus. You could say the Holy Spirit was on call 24 hours a day to help Peter and the others preach to the world! This was the great job Jesus had helped them prepare for from the very beginning. The disciples had now truly become fishers of men!

Many people become believers all because Peter and the others did God's will and followed Jesus' instructions. *"In their homes they broke bread and ate together. Their hearts were glad and honest and true. They praised God. They were respected by all the people. Every day the Lord added to their group those who were being saved" (Acts 2:46–47).* Soon the good news of Jesus spread to other towns and cities. All over the land believers joined together to worship and preach God's Word. In only a few short years, the disciples and the others that followed took Jesus' teachings beyond to other cities and kingdoms. The message was out and there was no stopping God's Word as people shared the good news with friends and strangers. Then his or her friends shared with someone else and so on, creating a people chain of sharing God's Word.

Passing on Jesus' teaching has continued all the way to us today! In fact we can be part of that chain, like Peter, by telling people about Jesus. We can spread the good news around our neighborhoods and beyond! We can work together to build God's church and make it grow!

When Jesus does return again, what a wonderful time it will be! Satan will be finished once and for all, and there will be no more sadness, pain, hunger, war, or sickness. Most importantly, we will be with Jesus and our heavenly Father forever. What could be better than that? Absolutely nothing is better than that! That's the best it can ever, ever be!

LET'S TALK:
Jesus told Nicodemus this, *"God loved the world so much that he gave his one and only Son. Anyone who believes in him will not die but will have eternal life"* (John 3:16). Jesus didn't come to earth to blame us or criticize us for all our mistakes and sins. He came to die so that our sins could be forgiven. Then we could be God's children again. Jesus died for everyone's sins, but each of us needs to ask God to forgive our sins and accept the importance of Jesus' death.

If you do something wrong and your parents are upset, you know they will forgive you. But remember, you still need to ask. It's the same with becoming God's child. Jesus already died for you and God will forgive you right away. But, you still need to ask. Nobody else can do it for you. God loves YOU!

Here's a prayer you can pray if you would like to accept God's gift.

Heavenly Father, I know that I have sinned,
And that you love me and sent
your only Son to earth to die on the cross for me.
Please forgive me my sins because Jesus died for me
And make me your child.
Now please help me to obey you and learn to do what is
right. Thank you!
In Jesus' name Amen!

When you pray that prayer, you become God's child. Remember Jesus is your Lord and your helper. Isn't that what God wanted from the very beginning? It sure was a long way to get back home, but Jesus has showed us the direct path right to His Father's house. God, Jesus, and the Holy Spirit are always on your side.

Now that you're God's child, you should talk to Him every day and learn more about the way He wants you to live your life. You get the answers by reading the Bible and going to church. And remember, God doesn't expect you to be perfect overnight. He just wants you to keep trying, learning, growing, and loving Him. God is always there to help, and He loves you more than you can imagine.

If you prayed the prayer at the end of the last story, congratulations! You are now God's child! Fill out the certificate below so that you'll always remember the wonderful day that you joined God's family.

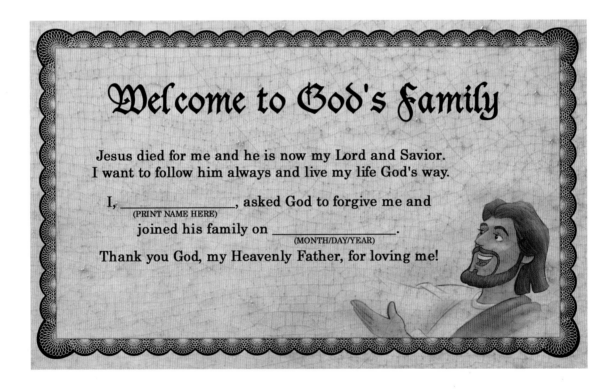

Welcome to God's Family

Jesus died for me and he is now my Lord and Savior.
I want to follow him always and live my life God's way.

I, _____, asked God to forgive me and
(PRINT NAME HERE)

joined his family on _____.
(MONTH/DAY/YEAR)

Thank you God, my Heavenly Father, for loving me!

FOCUS ON THE FAMILY®

Welcome to the Family!

We hope you've enjoyed this book. Heritage Builders was founded in 1995 by three fathers with a passion for the next generation. As a new ministry of Focus on the Family, Heritage Builders strives to equip, train, and motivate parents to become intentional about building a strong spiritual heritage.

It's quite a challenge for busy parents to find ways to build a spiritual foundation for their families—especially in a way they enjoy and understand. Through activities and participation, children can learn biblical truth in a way they can understand, enjoy—and remember.

Passing along a heritage of Christian faith to your family is a parent's highest calling. Heritage Builders' goal is to encourage and empower you in this great mission with practical resources and inspiring ideas that really work— and help your children develop a lasting love for God.

How To Reach Us

For more information, visit our Heritage Builders Web site! Log on to **www.heritagebuilders.com** to discover new resources, sample activities, and ideas to help you pass on a spiritual heritage. To request any of these resources, simply call Focus on the Family at 1-800-A-FAMILY (1-800-232-6459) or in Canada, call 1-800-661-9800. Or send your request to Focus on the Family, Colorado Springs, CO 80995. In Canada, write Focus on the Family, P.O. Box 9800, Stn. Terminal, Vancouver, B.C. V6B 4G3

To learn more about Focus on the Family or to find out if there is an associate office in your country, please visit www.family.org

We'd love to hear from you!

More Ways to Build Kids' Faith With These Great Resources from Heritage Builders and Focus on the Family!

Hugs in a Lunch Box Ages 5-7

These spiritually uplifting tear-out notes make it easy for parents to send their love throughout the day—whether children are at school, camp, or a sleepover! Children will be delighted and surprised to discover these reminders of the love God and their parents have for them! Included are 75 notes, plus stickers, Scripture verses, and notes for parents.

Hugs in a Lunch Box Ages 8-12

Just because they're growing up doesn't mean they won't appreciate finding an encouraging note in their lunchbox! More uplifting tear-out notes geared for older kids make it easy for parents to remind them they are loved. Included are 75 notes, plus stickers, Scripture verses, and notes for parents.

Bedtime Blessings 1 & 2

Strengthen the bond between parent and child with *Bedtime Blessings*. Written by best-selling author John Trent, Ph.D., these books offer countless ways to reaffirm the love God has for your child. Designed for children ages 7 and under, it's a wonderful way to develop a habit of speaking encouraging words and blessing just before children go to sleep.

Parents' Guide to the Spiritual Growth of Children

Building a foundation of faith in your children can be easy—and fun!—with help from the *Parents' Guide to the Spiritual Growth of Children*. Through simple and practical advice, this comprehensive guide shows you how to build a spiritual training plan for your family, and it explains what to teach your children at different ages.

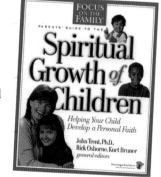

● ● ●

To request any of these resources, call Focus on the Family at
1-800-A-FAMILY (1-800-232-6459). In Canada, call 1-800-661-9800.
You may also write us at: Focus on the Family, Colorado Springs, CO 80995
In Canada, write to: Focus on the Family, P.O. Box 9800, Stn. Terminal, Vancouver, B.C. V6B 4G3
To learn more about Focus on the Family or to find out if we have an
associate office in your country, please visit www.family.org.
We'd love to hear from you!

Heritage
Builders®
Helping You Build a Family of Faith